Forex in nutshell:
Forex trading book for beginners

Gwen J. Allison

All rights reserved. No part of this publication may be reproduced, distributed, or transmitted in any form or by any means, including photocopying, recording, or other electronic or mechanical methods, without the prior written permission of the publisher, except in the case of brief quotations embodied in critical reviews and certain other noncommercial uses permitted by copyright law.

Copyright ©Gwen J. Allison, 2022.

COURSE IN FOREX TRADING

You may dive right into the thrilling world of online forex trading with the help of this EBook. The majority of the subjects are relevant to the FX market, however, some are also relevant to other markets.

Please be aware that this is not a comprehensive guide to internet trading. But the information provided here will give you the fundamentals you need to start trading in a manageable amount of time.

To follow along as subjects are covered, it is advised that you download a trading platform and create a demo account.

You just need a trading platform to learn alongside for the time being; any MT4 trading platform will do.

Everyone has a different learning curve, so be kind to yourself and take your time before you start trading in real-time with actual money.

Give yourself time to practise, and when you enter the wildly lucrative world of internet trading, your perseverance and patience will pay off for you!

CONTENTS

WHAT IS FOREX?
TERMINOLOGIES
CURRENCY PAIRS(PIPS, LOTS, QUOTE, LEVERAGE, BROKERS)
CANDLESTICKS(reversal candles)
SUPPORT AND RESISTANCE(dips, rallies)
TRENDLINES
CHART PATTERNS
BASICS OF ELLIOTT WAVES
INDICATORS
BASIC FUNDAMENTAL ANALYSIS: NEWS
TRADING BASICS: [buy, sell, stop loss, take profit, pending order]
RISK MANAGEMENT
TRADE MANAGEMENT
TRADING PLAN
A MODEL TRADING PLAN
COMBINING EVERYTHING

WHAT IS FOREX?

Forex is short for "Foreign Exchange."
It is the exchange of money (currency) between two parties in return for services. It simply refers to exchanging one currency for another with the intention of generating a profit in trade.

With daily trades totaling more than $6 trillion, forex is the biggest financial market in the world. No other market even approaches this volume.

In the forex market, currencies are always matched, thus we always trade two currency pairs at once. A few examples are EUR/USD, GBP/USD, USD/JPY, and USD/CHF.

The value of one currency rises as the value of the other falls. Two economies are reflected in this; as one economy grows, the second one recedes in proportion to the first.

Trading allows us to make money whether we buy or sell. Since the forex market is OTC (over-the-counter), which means there is no central marketplace, most trading takes place online, and all trading is transparent, we have access to it around-the-clock.

TERMINOLOGIES

When discussing deals, certain phrases tend to be utilised in the forex environment or the majority of financial markets:

- **MARKET:** The visual representation of pricing information for trading instruments on your trade charts.

- **TREND:** A currency pair's trend is its upward, downward, or sideways movement.

- **UPTREND:** when the market's value, or the price of a currency pair, is rising.

- **DOWNTREND:** when the market is losing value or moving down.

- **LONG:** This is when a currency pair is purchased.

- **SHORT:** when a currency is sold.

- **GOING LONG:** this means that you have purchased or are planning to purchase a currency pair.

- **GOING SHORT:** means that you have sold or intend to sell a currency pair.

- **BULL or BULLISH:** Means traders that purchase or trade uptrends

- **BEARS or BEARISH:** Means traders who are selling or trading downtrends

CURRENCY PAIRS

In the forex market, currencies are often shortened and given nicknames.

USD.
GBP.
EUR.
JPY.
AUD.
CHF.
NZD.
CAD.

These are the primary ones; there are many more.
United States Dollar (greenback, buck)
Great Britain pound (sterling)
Euro (euro)
Japanese Yen(yen) Australian Dollar (Aussie)

Swedish Franc (swiss) New Zealand Dollar (kiwi)
Canadian Dollar (loonie)
The most liquid and regularly traded currencies are simply referred to as major currencies. They are often associated with the US dollar.
Less is traded in crosses, and emerging countries use unusual currencies.

EUR/USD GBP/USD USD/CAD JPY/USD AUD/USD USD/CHF NZD/USD
GBP/JPY EUR/GBP EUR/CHF, NZD/CAD, AUD/CHF, etc.
CROSSES (Some) (Some)
EXOTICS (Some) (Some) Mexican Peso (USDMXN), Singapore Dollar (USDSGD), South African Rand (USDZAR), etc.

PIP

Profit or loss for each deal is calculated using the unit of price measurement used in foreign exchange.

For instance, if I purchase 1 (one) lot of EUR/USD at 1.1499 and the market rises to 1.1505, In other words, the price increases by 6 pips, and I made a profit of 6 pips, or $60.

LOT

We purchase and sell currency pairs in lots, or units of measurement, in the forex market. There are many sizes, including nano, micro, mini, and normal quantities.

To purchase a certain lot size, you need to have a certain sum of money. We refer to this as margin.

For illustration, let's say I'm using the leverage of 1:100 (more on that later):
The price of a micro lot is $1,000.
The cost of a small lot is $10,000.
It would cost $100,000 for a typical lot.
Your profit is determined by your lot size.
$0.1 per pip for a micro lot.
$1 per pip for a little lot.
$10 for a standard lot of pip
Values vary depending on the pairs.

QUOTE

A broker will provide you with a quotation to convey the price of a currency pair to you.

Example: GBP/USD 1.31044 1.31058 (Bid)
Ask is the selling price;
Bid is the purchase price.

You pay the price shown to acquire or sell that currency.

LEVERAGE

Consider how a little doily may move a massive and heavy item when used to swap a small bit of money for a much greater quantity. Brokers provide traders with leverage, which comes in multiple generous portions. If employed wisely, leverage allows traders to make huge sums of money.

If a trader uses leverage carelessly, they run the danger of losing all of their money.
Utilizes Sizes
1:50 1:100 1:200 1:400 1:500 1:1000
Earlier, we used the 1:100 leverage as an illustration. Take 1:400 as an illustration now

If I created an account with my broker utilizing a leverage ratio of 1:400 and had $1,000 in trading capital, it would equate to $400,000 ($1,000 multiplied by 400).

My broker will thus allow me to trade with my $1,000 as if I had more. a trading capital of $400,000.

Although you may be tempted to believe that using very high leverage is the secret to incredible fortune, doing so is often the quickest and riskiest way to lose all of your trading money. This is the reason why traders often advise clients to "only trade with the capital/money you are prepared to lose."
Note: I'll show you how to effectively control your risk even while utilizing

large leverage under "Risk/Trade Management."

BROKERS

Brokers serve as the intermediaries between buyers and sellers in the currency market. Brokers offer trading platforms on which you may make your trades, and in exchange, they are compensated each time you initiate a transaction via commissions or the so-called spread.

The spread is the discrepancy between a currency pair's ask and bid prices.
For instance, if your broker quoted you that you should buy EUR/USD at 1.1467 and sell it at 1.1470, it would indicate a 3 pip spread (70-67).
If you are just starting, it is a good idea to start with major currencies

since they often have the lowest spreads.

However, with a sound strategy and trading plan, discipline, and a little bit of experience, you can go on to trade pairs with greater gaps and still be successful.

There are many brokers available, so doing a little research is necessary to choose the best one.

I conduct most of my trading via brokers.
They provide ECN/STP accounts, have modest spreads, and are open and honest with their customers.

To learn more about this, speak with the representative of your broker.

On trading platforms, the charts may be shown in three different ways:
Line chart
Bar chart
Candlestick chart.

I won't go into detail on the other two since candlesticks will be used.

CANDLESTICKS

When displayed on charts, candlesticks are pictorial and simple to comprehend. They provide us with important market data at every time interval, whether it be minutes, hours, days, weeks, or months.

Candlesticks are so named because they resemble candles and often have "wicks" (the highest and lowest values) protruding from both ends. Each candle symbolizes a trading instrument's open, high, low, and closing prices during a certain period.

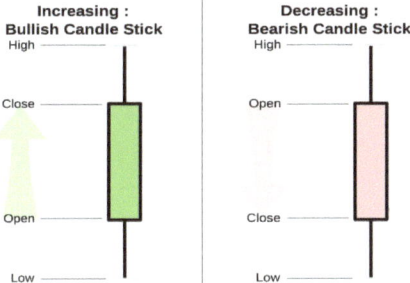

Candles make it easier for traders to assess the market visually, more quickly, and effectively. They also produce a variety of patterns that, if learned, may greatly benefit you while trading.

As buyers and sellers contend for dominance in the market, candles develop.

Over the years, this conflict has given rise to many forms, styles, and patterns; however, we will concentrate on only three candle types known as Reversal Candlesticks.

These tend to happen during market-turning moments when the trend reverses direction, making them rather significant.

(1) Hammer: may also be inverted; this specific candle formation is particularly strong since, most of the time, it turns the market in the opposite direction after an upward or downward trend.

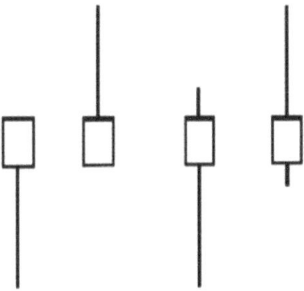

(2) Spinning Top comes in a variety of sizes and shapes and performs almost the same tasks as the hammer candle.

(3) Tweezers/Railway Tracks: These have two candles that are parallel to one another and made up of both a bullish and a bearish candle, thus their name.

When you see them towards the conclusion of a price run—upward or downward—they also turn around the trends.

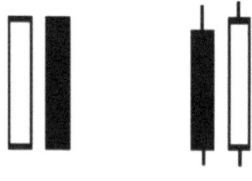

Railway Tracks/ Tweezers

Just concentrate on the fact that anytime you observe these specific candlestick patterns near the conclusion of an uptrend or downturn, anticipate a trend reversal to some extent.

SUPPORT AND RESISTANCE

A currency pair's support and resistance levels function as intangible floors and ceilings that restrict or accelerate price movement.

These activities are what causes price reversals or trend changes; when the price is going down, we refer to these regions as support, and when the price is moving up, we refer to them as resistance.

As a result, whether the trend is heading up or down when you look at a currency pair, the market often has a zigzag appearance because of the levels of support and resistance that slow or stop price movement.

This is very natural, and we may benefit from it by placing trades in these locations.
Let's imagine you want to join a buy trade when the market is in an uptrend (moving higher).

The ideal course of action is to wait patiently for the price to reach a resistance level, reverse, and then hit a support level before beginning to move upward once again.

In contrast, to place a sell order while the market is moving down, you must wait for the price to reach a level of support, reverse, then reach a level of resistance and continue moving down.

A trader who understands support and resistance will undoubtedly be highly successful since it is pretty much the key driver of how the markets move.

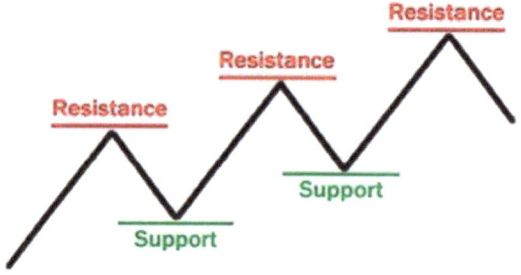

The graphic illustrates how support levels may change from resistance to support, and vice versa.

TRENDLINES

To indicate regions of support or resistance on your charts, trendlines are simple lines drawn diagonally above or below the price.

When these lines are breached, reversals may be predicted as well as the trend's direction.

Typically, trendlines are created around the highest or lowest points of at least two or more candlesticks or swing highs. You may design these lines using the drawing tools on any trading platform.

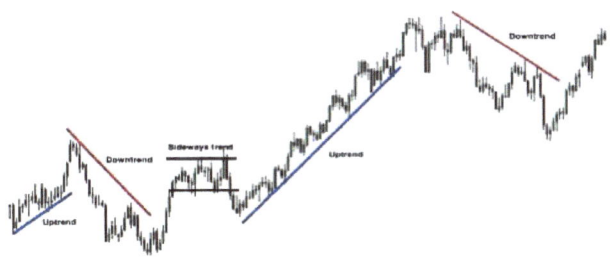

CHART PATTERNS

Over time, traders who studied the charts found that the markets moved in predictable cycles and patterns that were visible.

Time and time again. We refer to them as chart patterns. We have fantastic opportunities to profit from the markets when we can recognize these patterns.

Some patterns appear to support the trend while others seem to work against it. Here, we'll only pay attention to one reversal pattern.

While you are urged to learn the others independently, if you focus on learning just one for the duration of this course, you should be fine.

WAVE BOTTOM & WAVE TOP

Although I refer to this pattern in this course as Wave Top and Wave Bottom, the traditional name for it is 123 top or bottom.

WAVE TOP

When the price is nearing the end of an uptrend, it will reach a certain level of resistance that it will be unable to break through. Price will then attempt the level again, typically with lower volume, and collapse into a downtrend.

WAVE BOTTOM

formed when the price reaches a certain level of support to signal the end of a downtrend, reverses, and retries that level again with less force, and then surges higher in an uptrend. Because of this, watch for Wave Tops at the end of an uptrend and Wave Bottoms at the end of a downtrend.

A Wave Bottom can appear in the middle of an uptrend, and a Wave Top top can appear in the middle of a downtrend. Take note that these patterns can also appear in the middle of a move.

BASICS OF ELLIOTT WAVES

Ralph Nelson Elliott, an accountant, developed and popularized a theory he dubbed Waves in the middle the to late 1920s and 1930s. Waves were based on the idea that investors and the general public's psychology and emotions were what drove the stock market to move in a predictable and repeating way.

These waves may be recognized, and by doing so, market tops and bottoms and price direction could be precisely predicted.

He split these waves into Impulse waves and Corrective waves, and he proposed that the waves in a moving market occur in a 5-3 pattern. There are five impulse waves—also known

as motive waves—that follow the general trend—and three corrective waves.
2 and 4 correct the wave, whereas wave 1, 3, and 5 follow the general pattern.

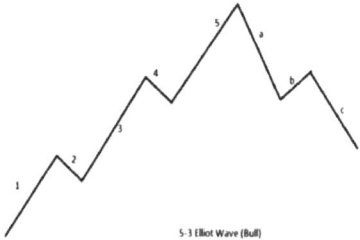

5-3 Eliot Wave (Bull)

Bullish and bearish markets both experience waves.

Since Elliott Waves is a complicated topic that needs lengthy study, I will only briefly touch on its fundamentals in this eBook. However, mastering this fundamental concept will transform your capacity to evaluate and predict where the market will go and how long it will stay there.

NOTE:
benefits from the Elliott Waves count, particularly from wave 3.
One of the motive waves—referred to as an Extension—usually stands out among the others, the motive waves 1, 3, and 5.

It has been found over time that wave 3 is often what happens, however, sometimes waves 1 or 5 may also be prolonged.
A, B, and C waves of correction.

The market corrects itself once the five waves are finished using three corrective waves, denoted by the letters a, b, and c. (refer to the diagram above).

Despite there being 24 different kinds of corrective wave patterns, there are only three that can be generalized:

Zigzag: Wave "b" in a zigzag pattern is often shorter than waves "a" or "c," and these waves tend to be quite steep.

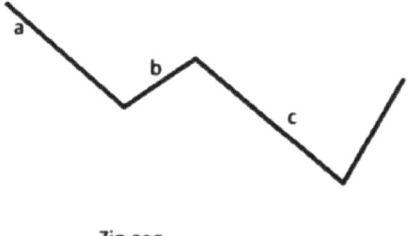

Zig-zag

Flat: Waves are usually the same height and tend to flow in one direction; this is what traders refer to as congestion, consolidation, or "a calm market."

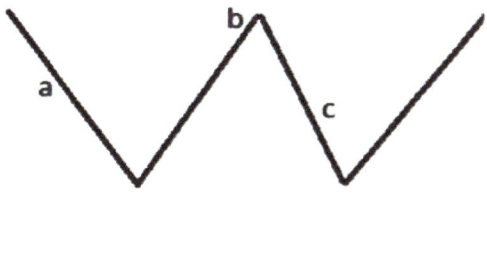

Flat

Triangle: These waves are symmetrical, ascending, or descending in formation, and they are constrained by trend lines that converge and diverge. This specific wave formation will be made easier for you by further studying chart patterns.

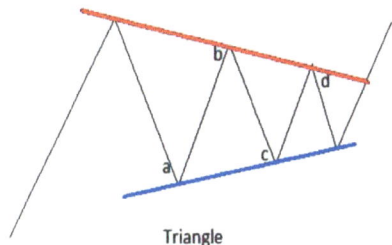

Triangle

Elliott Wave's "Three Cardinal Rules"

Any Elliott wave technician must adhere to and follow these three fundamental principles:

1) Wave 3 is never the shortest.

2) Wave 2 does not extend beyond Wave 1's beginning.

3) Wave 4 cannot enter the same space as wave 1 during its passage.

This is only a condensed overview of Elliott Wave Theory, as I said before, but if you commit to studying the charts and mastering the discipline of wave recognition and counting, you will benefit significantly.

A skilled Elliott Wave technician can only be attained via time and experience.

Do not worry if this portion makes you feel like you just downed a sack of bricks. If you don't get this all at once, you'll be alright. It becomes simpler with time with consistent practice.

The 5-3 wave pattern may be seen in the markets in the following instances.

5-3 Elliot wave(bull)

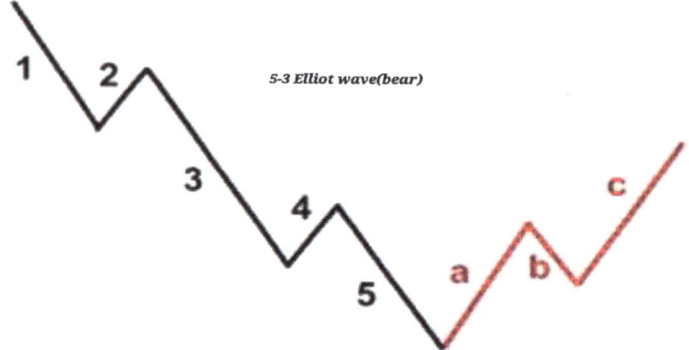
5-3 Elliot wave(bear)

Elliott Wave Principle by A.J. Frost and Robert Prechter is a good book to read for more research.

INDICATORS

These are instruments that traders use, as the name suggests, to assist them in making defensible choices on the market's direction. Indicators that are either leading or lagging might be used to classify them.

Since lagging indicators' calculations are based on historical price data, they often lag behind price movement or follow it. Leading indicators, on the other hand, anticipate market direction or activity somewhat before price.

There are lots of them, each one specifically created by traders to meet their needs and goals. Every indication has advantages and disadvantages, but in the end, a trader's use of an indicator will determine how effectively it works. Just two of them will be examined.

I) **MOVING AVERAGES (EXPONENTIAL)**:

The price movement is slowed down and the trend is followed with the aid of moving averages.

They lag as they are dependent on historical price data, but they are useful in identifying trends and probable locations of support and resistance.

I use EMA 21, 5, and 55. By emphasising more current price data, EMAs lessen the lag.

II) MOVING AVERAGE CONVERGENCE DIVERGENCE (M.A.C.D):

Driving Average Convergence With the aid of the 12, 26, and 9 moving averages, the divergence indicator tracks price movement and alerts traders when a new trend is about to start.

Trend change may be indicated by the signal line's passing over or under the trigger line.

The MACD, however, is a lagging indicator and performs better on charts with a greater period.

Although we won't be focused on it in my approach, it is a highly valuable signal for spotting divergence in trader and market mood.

You should look up "MACD Divergence" and read some information about it, however; you'll find it to be quite helpful.

BASIC FUNDAMENTAL ANALYSIS: NEWS

Before I started trading, I learned that traders used either technical analysis or fundamental analysis to make trading decisions.

Technical analysis is trading with the aid of technical indicators, tools, and speculative analysis based on price action on charts, whereas fundamental analysis examines the socioeconomic factors that drive an economy or economies and uses them to predict the future direction of a currency pair (or any other trading instrument).

Although I mostly trade using technical analysis, I do keep track of important news events, avoid the markets before they happen, and look for trading chances thereafter, usually an hour or two later.

Although it is debatable if all traders who trade the news have a valid purpose for doing so, doing so is stressful and hazardous since it may cause the market to whipsaw violently and without prior notice or rhyme or reason when trader emotions change in response to the news.

Even while you may find a suitable balance with a little study if necessary, most news events won't have a significant negative impact on your trades if you are a technical trader and trade on high-level charts (4 hours and above).

News can be found on websites like www.dailyfx.com, www.forexfactory.com, Bloomberg, and CNBC, and these days, the majority of brokers provide news event alerts immediately on their trading interfaces.

TRADING BASICS

This following set of instructions ought to be simple for you since you should have become a little familiar with your MT4 trading software by this point.

The time of day is something to consider when you wish to trade.

The best trading times are often in between the London and US sessions.

Ask your broker about the market open and closure timings since they might vary depending on where you are.

SETTING UP ORDERS ON YOUR TRADING PLATFORM

- **HOW TO BUY**: The three most popular methods are to hit the F9 key, pick "New Order" from the toolbar menu, or right-click on the chart and choose "New Trade."

- **HOW TO SELL**: Simply click "sell" and follow the same steps as before.

- **STOP LOSS**: This is an order you make that automatically exits a losing trade at a certain level, saving you from losing all of your cash or funds.

In a bullish trade, you position it below your entrance price and, if feasible, below the most recent level of support; in a bearish trade, you place it above your original entry price and the most recent level of resistance.

- **TAKE PROFIT:** This is an order you make that instantly ends your

    When it hits a certain predefined price level or profit objective, it will trade for a profit.

    If at all feasible, you put it above your entry price at a specified level of resistance in a bullish trade and below your entry price at a planned level of support in a bearish trade.

- **MARKET ORDER**: When you click to purchase or sell at the current price that your broker is offering, this is the order that is placed. You may enter the transaction immediately and it is instantaneous
- **PENDING ORDER**: A pending order is one that you place at the price of your choice. It can only be filled when the market changes in your favor. There are many different kinds, but the most popular are purchase stop, buy limit, sale stop, and sell limit.

1. **Buy Stop**: put above the current market price to buy.

2. **Buy Limit**: set below the going rate to buy.

3. **Sell Stop**: positioned below the going price with the intention of selling.

4. **Sell Limit:** set above the current price with the intention of selling.

RISK MANAGEMENT

Long-term success as a trader will depend on how you manage your trading funds. The magnitude of the percentage you should risk for every transaction should decrease as your investment amount increases.

Avoid putting more than 2% of your trading money at risk in a single deal. For instance, if trader A deposits $5000 into a broker's trading account, he shouldn't take on more risk than [(2100)5000]=100.

So, each trade's stop loss amount shouldn't be more than $100. His lot size will vary depending on the leverage he is using and the number of pips he chooses to stake every transaction.

It is ultimately up to you how much danger you want to take. The most experienced and confident traders may choose to risk more each transaction, whilst the cautious traders may choose to risk as little as.5%.

To gain confidence and prevent an emotional rollercoaster while trading, beginners should keep to the 2% guideline.

I already discussed leverage; although it is true that the lower your leverage, the less your risk, you may need to utilize larger leverage if your trading capital is insufficient to allow you to acquire lots to trade with.

For instance, a trader with a $200 beginning capital may pick leverage of

400:1 or greater and still practice prudent risk management and turn a profit.

A trader of this kind will first trade micro-lots until his account is big enough to trade mini lots, and then finally regular lots.

Because he is completely aware of what he is doing, an experienced trader may also utilize the 1:400 leverage to create a much bigger account, such as $10,000, and earn enormous gains.

When applying leverage, use caution and start cautiously. You should focus more on placing effective transactions than trying to make a killing on each one since you can lose everything much sooner than you anticipate.

Trading is all about shifting the odds in your favor, thus if a trader uses a method with a success percentage of 60–70%, he may still be profitable each month provided he follows his strategy.

Say you only engage in deals with a 3:1 profit-to-risk ratio (you risk 1 dollar to make 3 dollars.). Even if you made 10 deals and lost seven of them, you would still make money (3*3=9; 7*1=7).

So long as you use solid risk management, everything will be OK.

TRADE MANAGEMENT

Right now, the transaction is going your way. How do you behave? Due to improper trade management, the majority of traders wind up losing money on their deals. Once you've placed your trades, you must manage them properly to prevent winning trades from becoming bad. You may use the advice below:

1) Always set stop losses and take profit levels before each transaction.

2) Keep your stops just far enough away from your entry point to give your trade room to breathe without being stopped out, but not too far away. If you're a day trader, 20–30 pip will often be plenty.

From the moment of entrance, or below the crossover of the EMA 21 and 5, which I discuss in my course, put your stop below the previous or current support level when in a long trade (buying).

Put your stop above the previous or current resistance level from where you entered when you are in a short position (selling).

3) To safeguard your money while trade is active and the price has increased in your favor by at least 15 to 20 pip, move your stop to the price at which you entered the transaction.

I can't emphasize this enough: Most traders lose money for this one reason. Your money is secure even if the market falls again and wipes you out.

Since the price will often continue to rise, you may now trail your stop every certain number of pips (ten, fifteen, twenty, or another number of your choosing) until your take profit is reached or you are stopped out.

These are the only actions you should do to continue trading effectively.

You would be wise to internalize these guidelines and, more importantly, to always put them into practice while trading.

TRADING PLAN

Now that you have everything you need in your toolbox, you want to put it all to use for you. Introducing the trading strategy.

A trading strategy may be a set of guidelines or a to-do list that you strictly adhere to for each deal you make. This significantly lowers emotional trading and offers you the advantage you need to be successful.

No trading method is flawless; their efficacy typically ranges from 60% to 80%. However, a trader who creates and adheres to a trading plan may raise trading efficiency and success to as much as 95%, if not higher!

So how does one create a trading strategy? The fundamental idea is that a trading strategy should be a collection of rules in keeping with your trading system, style, and personality that you follow precisely and with discipline EVERY SINGLE TIME. It will vary from trader to trader since we all have distinct features and aims.

Here is a trading strategy you may use as an example. Examine it and modify it to fit your preferences and objectives.

A MODEL TRADING PLAN

1) SEEK SETUPS ON LONGER TIME FRAMES, PRIMARILY ON DAILY, 4-HOUR, AND 1-HOUR CHARTS. TO DETERMINE TRADE BIAS FOR THE DAY, ENGAGE IN TOP-DOWN ANALYSIS FROM THE MONTHLY DOWN TO THE 1-HOUR TIME FRAME.

2) ENTER TRADE VIA THE LOWER TIME FRAMES, 1HR, 30MIN, 15MIN, ONCE YOU HAVE CAST-IRON SETUPS.

3) ONLY CHECK FOR EMA AND MACD CROSSOVER/BOUNCE AS ONE SET UP

4) TRADE MOST OF THE TIME WITH THE PRESENT TREND.

5) ONE TRADE AT A TIME, INSIDE THE 2% MARGIN, REGARDLESS OF HOW MANY GOOD SETUPS THERE ARE!

6) SEARCH ALL AVAILABLE PAIRS, SELECT THE MOST SENSIBLE AND VIABLE SETUP, AND LEAVE AWAY ANY CONFUSING SETUP!

7) AVOID TRADE SETUPS THAT ARE CURRENTLY IN MOTION AS THEY HAVE A PROPENSITY TO REWARD YOU!

Notice I didn't mention how many pip targets to set for each transaction.

Although the decision to set profit objectives for each transaction is yours, the Profit Target Calculator may help.

If you are inclined to do so, you may decide to set a goal amount of pip every transaction or simply choose a certain target level and adhere to it.

COMBINING EVERYTHING

Now that you virtually have everything you need, you may start working as a trader.

Learning a trading system or strategy is the next stage.

You will be successful if you adhere to the guidelines and standards as simply as possible.

You'll soon see an improvement your trading if you put in at least an hour of practice each trading day to start getting a sense of how currencies move.

www.ingramcontent.com/pod-product-compliance
Lightning Source LLC
Chambersburg PA
CBHW040325220526
45473CB00009B/2568